MW00946617

Matthew Perry

Biography

The Whole Story

Timely Press

Table of Contents

Copyright Notice

All rights reserved.

Copyright © 2024 by Timely Press.

Introduction

Matthew Perry. The name conjures up images of a wisecracking jester, a master of the sarcastic quip, a beacon of dry wit in the coffee-fueled chaos of Central Perk. In the classic comedy "Friends," he played Chandler Bing, who captured hearts and spurred laughter, becoming synonymous with the show's infectious charisma. But Perry's story is more than just a punchline; it's a tapestry woven with resilience, vulnerability, and a relentless pursuit of laughter, both on screen and in the face of life's harshest realities.

Born in 1969, Perry's journey began in the quaint town of Williamstown, Massachusetts. His childhood, however, was a canvas for change. His parents' separation led him across the border, where he found a new home amidst the maple leaves and chilly winds of Ottawa, Canada. Here, he befriended a young Justin Trudeau, little knowing their paths would diverge, one towards comedy and the other towards the halls of Parliament.

Tennis became his early muse. He dominated junior circuits, dreams of Grand Slams dancing in his head. But fate had other plans. At 15, he traded snow-dusted courts for the sun-kissed streets of Los Angeles, joining his father, a successful actor. Tennis, once a source of triumph, faltered under the Californian sun. Its fading echo, however, fueled a new passion: acting.

The Buckley School's stage became his proving ground. He devoured scripts, honed his comedic timing, and discovered the intoxicating power of making people laugh. From high school plays to bit parts in sitcoms, Perry's journey was a slow climb, paved with rejections and missed opportunities. But he persevered, fueled by an insatiable hunger for recognition, for success, and for the spotlight.

Then, in 1994, lightning struck. A quirky ensemble sitcom called "Friends" premiered, catapulting Perry and his castmates into the stratosphere of fame. Chandler Bing, the sarcastic wordsmith with a heart of gold, became his alter ego. The world laughed with him, at him, and, most importantly, because of him. Yet, beneath the surface of Chandler's witty one-liners, a hidden battle raged.

Perry's addiction to painkillers, a demon spawned companion since his teenage years, reared its ugly head during "Friends'" meteoric rise. The pressures of fame, the constant scrutiny, the whirlwind of success—they became the perfect storm, fueling a dependence that threatened to engulf him.

He got into rehab in 1997 and then again in 2001, at the height of the show's success. The journey back was arduous, paved with relapses and the constant tug-of-war between the man he wanted to be and the darkness that threatened to consume him. But Perry, fueled by an unyielding spirit, refused to surrender. He returned to the set, to Chandler, and to the laughter that resonated with millions. Perry estimates spending more than $9 million on sobriety efforts.

This is just the beginning of Perry's story, a complex narrative that transcends the confines of a sitcom set. It's a proof of the human spirit's ability to weather storms, to find humor in the face of adversity, and to laugh even when the world seems determined to make you cry.

In the chapters to come, we'll delve deeper into Perry's battles, his triumphs, and the man behind the mask of the sarcastic jester. We'll see how his experiences shaped his philanthropy, his relationships, and, sadly, his untimely death.

Chapter 1

A Life Between Two Shores

Matthew Perry's life began under a double star sign: fame and abandonment. Perry's birthdate is August 19, 1969, in Massachusetts. The paparazzi's flashing cameras, drawn to his father, the well-known actor, announced his presence. But before his first breath could fully inflate his tiny lungs, the cameras clicked shut, capturing the image of a broken home. His parents, caught in the whirlwind of their careers, couldn't hold onto their love, leaving Matthew adrift on a sea of unspoken promises.

His childhood became a tapestry woven from two distinct threads: the bustling, vibrant city of Ottawa, where his mother, a beauty queen turned journalist, rose to become the press secretary to the Canadian Prime Minister, and the sun-drenched streets of Los Angeles, where his father chased the golden dream of Hollywood. Though his mother remarried, the warmth of his stepfather, Keith Morrison, a renowned journalist himself, couldn't quite mend the cracks in Matthew's heart. He felt like a lone sail, perpetually caught between two shores, never quite belonging to either.

The world saw a bright, precocious child, a whirlwind of energy and mischief. But within, a storm brewed. Matthew's early years were marked by a gnawing sense of abandonment. He lashed out, crying out for attention and morphing into misbehavior—stolen trinkets, plumes of smoke from forbidden cigarettes, and grades that nosedived like a plane with a faulty engine.

His father, a distant yet ever-present figure glimpsed on flickering TV screens and glossy magazine covers, became a symbol of everything he craved and missed. "I saw his face more often on TV or in magazines than I did in reality," Matthew would later write. "But he was my hero." This bittersweet admiration painted his childhood in shades of longing, a constant yearning for a connection that never quite materialized.

Even as a baby, Matthew's world was tinged with turmoil. He was a restless child, plagued by colic, and his cries were often soothed with barbiturates, a potent cocktail of chemicals that numbed not just the pain but, perhaps, a part of his nascent sense of self. This early exposure to mind-altering substances would become a recurring theme in his later years, a desperate attempt to silence the whispers of abandonment that echoed in his soul.

At a younger age of 13, Matthew took his first tentative steps down a path that would become a perilous dance with oblivion—alcohol. It was a bitter elixir, an attempt to drown the pain of feeling unmoored and of being a satellite forever orbiting a distant sun. This thirst for solace would become a constant companion, a dark shadow lurking at the edges of his triumphs.

His education, in a way, embodied the disarray of his existence. While attending Rockcliffe Park Public School in Canada, known for its regimented environment, he struggled to excel academically. He had issues as a kid, sometimes beating up his fellow classmates, among them Justin, the son of Trudeau, who is now the Prime Minister of Canada.

Notably, tennis. He was natural on the court, his agile limbs weaving a silent symphony of power and precision.

Perry journeyed to Los Angeles to join his father. The once-confident athlete found himself stumbling on unfamiliar turf. The competition in Los Angeles was fierce, like a shark tank where raw talent wasn't enough. He felt like a deflated balloon, his confidence pricked by the relentless sunshine and the mocking stares of his peers.

Yet, amidst the shadows of doubt, a flicker of hope ignited. At Buckley School, a beacon of academic rigor nestled amidst the palm trees, Matthew discovered a hidden passion—acting. The stage became his sanctuary, a place where he could shed the skin of his insecurities and slip into the vibrant costumes of a thousand different lives. He devoured scripts with the same ferocity he once reserved for tennis balls, his tongue tripping over unfamiliar monologues with a newfound joy. His nights were spent at L.A. Connection, where laughter became his currency and the stage his playground.

As the curtain fell on his high school years, Matthew Perry stood on the precipice of adulthood. He was a mixture of contradictions—a troubled child with a yearning for connection, a failed athlete with a newfound passion, a lonely soul with a mischievous glint in his eye. He was ready to step onto the grand stage of life, his script still being written, his lines yet to be learned, but his heart overflowing with a fierce determination to find his place in the world, one laugh, one tear, one character at a time.

Chapter 2

From Sidekick to Spotlight

Matthew Perry, fresh-faced and ambitious, stepped onto the Hollywood stage, eager to share his comedic gift with the world. But the spotlight wasn't always focused on him. Early days were filled with the hustle of auditions, the sting of rejections, and the bittersweet comfort of playing the sidekick. Yet, with each stumble, he honed his craft, building a toolkit of humor that would soon have audiences roaring with laughter.

His first taste of the silver screen came in 1988, in a supporting role in "A Night in the Life of Jimmy Reardon." Sharing the screen with the rising star River Phoenix was a thrill, but the film's impact was fleeting. Television, however, beckoned with its promise of weekly laughs and familiar faces.

In 1987, Perry landed his first sitcom, "Second Chance." The premise was unique: a man gets to relive his teenage years with the help of his future self. Unfortunately, the audience wasn't as intrigued as the writers, and the show was soon retooled, focusing solely on Perry's character and rebranded as "Boys Will Be Boys." Despite the name change, the ratings remained stubbornly low, and the show met its untimely demise.

But Perry, never one to give up, bounced back with the resilience of a seasoned boxer. He took on guest roles in shows like "Empty Nest" and "Growing Pains," honing his comedic timing and showcasing his undeniable charm. He even dipped his toes into the world of biopics, playing the dashing Desi Arnaz Jr. in "Call Me Anna," adding a touch of musical swagger to his repertoire.

Still, the siren song of sitcom success continued to call. In 1993, he took the lead in "Home Free," portraying a young reporter navigating the chaotic world of journalism. While the show had its highlights, it struggled to captivate the audience and eventually faded into obscurity on television. Undeterred, Perry ventured into the realm of sci-fi with the pilot for "LAX 2194," a futuristic airport drama that, like many promising pilots, never took flight.

These were the years of hustle, of chasing that elusive "big break" with the relentless determination of a terrier chasing a tennis ball. Each audition was a gamble, and each rejection was a sting, but Perry learned from every setback. He honed his craft, refined his comedic persona, and built a network of friends and mentors in the industry. He discovered that Hollywood was a marathon, not a sprint, and he was in for the long haul.

In the middle of these early struggles, there were glimpses of the brilliance to come. In a poignant episode of "Growing Pains," he delivered a heartbreaking performance as a young man who dies in a drunk-driving accident. It was a powerful display of his dramatic range, a hint at the depth that lay beneath the surface of his comedic persona.

This period also saw the seeds of his future philanthropy being sown. He volunteered at a homeless shelter, connecting with those less fortunate and discovering a sense of purpose beyond the glitz and glamour of Hollywood.

So, while the early chapters of Perry's story may not be filled with blockbuster successes and awards galore, they are crucial to understanding the man he became. These years of resilience, of learning through trial and error, shaped his character and laid the foundation for the meteoric rise that was just around the corner.

Chapter 3

Six Friends and One Coffeehouse

The year was 1994. New York City buzzed with a symphony of honking cabs and bustling dreams, and amidst the concrete jungle, six strangers were about to embark on a journey that would redefine the landscape of television comedy. Among them was Matthew Perry, a young actor with a wit as sharp as a freshly brewed espresso, ready to step into the shoes of a character who would become synonymous with sarcasm and self-deprecating humor—Chandler Bing.

The audition for "Friends" was a nerve-wracking affair, a pressure cooker where comedic timing and chemistry with the other hopefuls were the ingredients for success. But Perry, with his trademark dry humor and a smile that could melt the iciest heart, landed the role like a seasoned chef crafting the perfect dish.

Chandler Bing, the sarcastic maestro of witty one-liners, became Perry's alter ego. He was the sarcastic glue that held the group together, the voice of reason that often got lost in translation, and the hopeless romantic who, beneath the layers of jokes, yearned for a connection that wouldn't end in a disastrous punchline.

The magic of "Friends," however, wasn't just about Chandler's witty repartee. It was the undeniable chemistry of the entire cast—a six-pack of comedic geniuses who, on and off-screen, became a family bound by laughter and shared dreams. They celebrated each other's successes, mourned their rejections, and navigated the treacherous waters of fame with a bond that resonated with audiences across generations.

"Friends" wasn't just a sitcom; it was a cultural phenomenon. It redefined fashion trends with "The Rachel," made coffee shops the coolest hangout spots, and turned catchphrases like "Could I BE any more...?" into linguistic currency. It explored relationships, careers, and the messy realities of life with a lighthearted touch and a generous sprinkle of humor, mirroring the struggles and triumphs of millions of viewers.

For Perry, the success of "Friends" brought a whirlwind of change. His face showed up on billboards and magazine covers, and he became a household name. Fortune smiled upon him, but the pressures of fame and constant scrutiny took their toll. He battled with addiction throughout the show's run, a hidden struggle that threatened to engulf the man behind the laughs.

Yet Perry persevered. He sought help, found solace in his friends and family, and learned to navigate the treacherous terrain of fame with grace and resilience. He continued to pour his heart and soul into Chandler Bing, evolving the character from a sarcastic jokester to a man capable of love, vulnerability, and genuine tenderness.

As "Friends" neared its final curtain, Chandler and Monica's love story became the show's emotional anchor. Their journey from wisecracking roommates to devoted partners resonated deeply, a testament to the show's ability to grow with its audience and tackle deeper themes without sacrificing its signature humor.

"Friends" said goodbye to the world in May 2004, following 10 seasons of laughter, tears, and endless cups of coffee. It left behind a legacy that would continue to inspire and entertain, a testament to the power of friendship, humor, and the enduring charm of six friends navigating life, one hilarious quip at a time.

Chapter 4

Beyond Central Perk

While Rachel may have dreamed of Paris, Matthew Perry's post-"Friends" journey took him on a different kind of global exploration – a voyage through the diverse landscapes of acting. Having mastered the art of sitcom wit with Chandler Bing, he set his sights on new horizons, proving that his talent extended far beyond the confines of Central Perk's orange couch.

Perry's comedic charm remained a potent weapon, but he wielded it with greater nuance in films like "Fools Rush In" and "The Whole Nine Yards." In the former, he shed the sarcastic persona to play Eddie, a lovable but clueless architect who falls for Salma Hayek's free-spirited Isabel. Their cross-cultural clash provided fertile ground for humor, showcasing Perry's ability to elicit laughs while navigating genuine emotional depth. "The Whole Nine Yards," meanwhile, saw him reunite with Bruce Willis, their comedic chemistry playing off the absurdity of a gangster's witness-protection program gone wildly wrong. These roles proved that Perry's comedic timing was a passport to success, granting him access to both romantic lightheartedness and action-packed farce.

But Perry wasn't afraid to experiment beyond the realm of laughter. He got into the world of guest appearances, sprinkling his comedic magic on shows like "Scrubs" and "Will & Grace." In "Scrubs," he donned a doctor's coat to play Murray, a sarcastic surgeon with a secret soft spot, reminding us of Chandler's hidden vulnerability beneath the layers of jokes. On "Will & Grace," he turned up as Rachel's love interest, proving his talent for chemistry extended beyond Monica Geller. These glimpses into different comedic universes showcased Perry's versatility and his willingness to take risks, even if it meant playing in someone else's sandbox for a few laughs.

However, the true breadth of Perry's talent shone brightest when he embraced dramatic challenges. In "The West Wing," he donned a suit and a serious demeanor to portray Joe Quincy, a political consultant brought in to save the President's re-election campaign. Perry's sharp wit translated seamlessly to the world of political maneuvering, his character displaying both ruthless ambition and a hidden moral compass. This Emmy-nominated performance cemented his ability to command attention in dramatic roles, demonstrating that Perry could go toe-to-toe with seasoned political drama veterans.

He took this dramatic momentum even further in "The Ron Clark Story," playing the real-life teacher Ron Clark, who transformed a troubled inner-city classroom with unorthodox methods and unwavering dedication. Perry did a tour-de-force performance, capturing Clark's tough love approach with both intensity and compassion. This role earned him widespread critical acclaim and another Emmy nomination, solidifying his status as a dramatic actor capable of commanding the screen with nuanced emotional portrayals.

Matthew Perry's post-"Friends" journey wasn't just about breaking free from Chandler Bing's shadow; it was about exploring the full spectrum of his artistic palette. He traversed genres, embraced challenges, and proved that his talent resided not just in expertly crafted punchlines but in the depths of human emotion.

Chapter 5

Fools Rush in Project

As the credits rolled on the final episode of Friends, Matthew Perry wasn't ready to hang up his acting apron just yet. He craved stories beyond the cozy embrace of Central Perk—ones that stretched his wings and explored different shades of emotion. One film that fit the bill perfectly was "Fools Rush In," a romantic comedy that plunged him into the whirlwind of love, family, and cultural clashes.

Perry traded his sarcastic Chandler Bing persona for Alex Whitman, a straight-laced New Yorker sent to oversee the construction of a Vegas nightclub. Enter Isabel Fuentes, a free-spirited photographer who captures both his eye and his heart with her infectious laughter and vibrant spirit. One sizzling night later, a connection sparks, but fate throws a curveball in the form of three unexpected words: "I'm pregnant."

Isabel, determined to raise the child on her own, throws out an invitation: meet my family. Alex, drawn by both responsibility and a growing fondness for Isabel, takes the plunge. The cultural clash explodes like fireworks: salsa music battling bagels, traditional remedies colliding with modern medicine. Yet, amidst the awkwardness, a tender bond blooms, leading to a hasty Vegas wedding fueled by tequila and a shared desire to make things work.

But reality's alarm clock isn't silenced by confetti. Back in New York, Alex juggles career pressure with marital obligations, secretly accepting a new project that keeps him glued to his phone even while snuggled next to Isabel. The secret unravels, igniting a fiery argument that exposes the cracks in their fragile foundation.

As if scripted by a mischievous sitcom writer, complications arise. Isabel experiences a medical scare, leading her to push Alex away, shielding him from the possibility of heartbreak. He, misinterpreting her silence, retreats to New York, the distance echoing the growing chasm between them.

Meanwhile, in Mexico, Isabel grapples with motherhood, mourning the love she thought she had. With a heavy heart, she files for divorce, the final blow that pushes Alex towards a stark realization: his life is incomplete without Isabel and their little one.

Driven by newfound clarity and a heart full of longing, Alex embarks on a desperate chase. He follows clues, chasing rumors, until his path converges with Isabel's at the majestic Hoover Dam. Just as he confesses his undying love, fate takes another surprising turn – Isabel goes into labor.

In a surreal, poignant dance of life and love, their divorce papers arrive as their daughter takes her first breath. In a testament to their enduring connection, they chose to rewrite their story. Atop a cliff overlooking the awe-inspiring Grand Canyon, they exchange vows again, not as fools rushing in but as two hearts inextricably bound, ready to face life's adventures together, one laugh, one tear, one salsa step at a time.

"Fools Rush In" wasn't just a movie for Perry; it was a stepping stone on his post-"Friends" journey. It showcased his ability to navigate between humor and heartfelt emotion, playing a character who stumbles and learns, who embraces vulnerability, and who grows with each misstep. It allowed him to explore the complexities of love, the beauty of family, and the unwavering power of second chances, proving that sometimes the biggest fools are the ones who take the bravest leaps of faith.

Chapter 6

The Whole Nine Yards

Matthew Perry, fresh from Central Perk, traded sarcastic quips for shifty grins as Oz Oseransky in "The Whole Nine Yards," a comedy that blurred the lines between neighborly kindness and international mayhem. Oz, a mild-mannered dentist, finds his life uprooted when Jimmy "the Tulip" Tudeski, a notorious hitman, becomes his next-door neighbor.

Jimmy, with his slick charm and penchant for tulips, is everything Oz isn't. But when Oz's shrewish wife, Sophie, throws him under the mob bus, Oz becomes Jimmy's unwilling informant. Torn between loyalty and self-preservation, Oz finds himself entangled in a web of deception and danger, with bullets whizzing past faster than a dental drill.

Amidst the chaos, Oz develops a soft spot for Jimmy's estranged wife, Cynthia. She's the antithesis of Sophie—a breath of fresh air in Oz's whirlwind life. He vows to protect her, a promise that takes him across the border to Canada, where Jimmy's latest hit targets both a mob boss and Cynthia herself.

The plot thickens faster than tartar buildup when Oz discovers his own assistant, Jill, is a closet contract killer with a penchant for ice picks. He navigates a treacherous game of cat and mouse, witnessing Jimmy's brutal efficiency as he eliminates his enemies in a hail of bullets.

Oz, however, isn't content to be a mere pawn. He hatches a bold plan to end the bloodshed. He convinces Jimmy to fake his death by swapping teeth with an undercover detective, leaving the authorities to assume both the hitman and mob boss are deceased. Oz's daring gamble pays off, and Sophie and her scheming mother land in jail for their own murderous scheme, their recorded conversation providing irrefutable evidence.

With the dust settling, Cynthia inherits a hefty $10 million, a reward for Jimmy's "demise." But Jimmy, surprisingly, offers Oz and Cynthia a million each, a gesture driven by a newfound appreciation for family and, dare we say, love. Oz sees a genuine change in the "Tulip," his heart softening to the reformed hitman.

However, one final twist remains. Jimmy, reverting to his old ways, shoots Frankie, a loose end, before sparing Oz's life, attributing his uncharacteristic mercy to the power of love. The film ends with Jill testing Cynthia's loyalty, but she rejects the offer, choosing Oz and their newfound life. As Cynthia and Oz embrace, dancing amidst the chaos they so narrowly escaped, one thing is certain: in the world of "The Whole Nine Yards," even the mildest dentist can blossom into a tango-dancing hero, dodging bullets and finding love amidst the tulips.

Perry's portrayal of Oz, a timid man thrown headfirst into a world of gangsters and gore, is a comedic masterclass. He navigates the absurdity with perfect timing, his wide-eyed fear contrasting hilariously with Jimmy's nonchalant brutality. In "The Whole Nine Yards," Matthew Perry proves that his talent extends far beyond sarcastic punchlines, showcasing his charisma and versatility in a film that's as hilarious as it is suspenseful, reminding us that sometimes the best way to survive a life of crime is to laugh in the face of it, one tango step at a time.

Chapter 7

Wrestling with the Big Terrible Thing

While Chandler Bing brought laughter and romance to the small screen, Matthew Perry faced his own personal struggles off-camera. Addiction, the "big terrible thing," as he called it, cast a long shadow over his golden years on "Friends." It wasn't a sudden storm, but a slow, insidious creep that began before the coffeehouse laughs and ended up taking center stage in his personal narrative.

The whispers started with alcohol, a teenage escape that blossomed into a daily companion by the time Perry was 18. By the time "Friends" took off, the crutch had become a dependence, a way to conceal the pressures of fame and the uncertainties of life. But it was a 1997 jet-skiing accident that introduced a new, more potent villain: painkillers.

Vicodin, prescribed to dull the pain, became a seductive demon. The occasional pill morphed into a daily ritual, then a relentless craving. At his worst, Perry swallowed a staggering 55 pills a day, his body shrinking to a skeletal 128 pounds. The man making millions laugh was a prisoner of his own addiction, his brilliant wit clouded by a chemical haze.

"Friends" became a blur, seasons 3 through 6 shrouded in fog. He hid his secret behind forced smiles and witty lines, a master of camouflage for the unsuspecting world. But to his fellow castmates, the penguins, as he fondly called them, the cracks were visible. They offered support and a hand to hold in the darkness, but ultimately, only Perry could fight his own monsters.

He tried, oh, how he tried. Fifteen trips to rehab, each a desperate attempt to reclaim his life. Detox programs, therapy, alternative approaches—Perry threw everything at the wall, fueled by a flickering flame of hope and a gnawing fear.

The turning point, ironically, came from a conversation about another drug, oxycontin. His therapist, in a stark warning, described the devastating effects as a chilling echo of Perry's own journey. It was a jolting wake-up call, a moment of clarity that crystallized his determination.

This time, the fight was different. He embraced a holistic approach, mending his mind and body alongside professional treatment. Meditation, exercise, and healthy eating—Perry rebuilt himself brick by brick, refusing to surrender to the demons that had once held him captive.

The path wasn't smooth. Relapses lurked, tempting him back into the familiar abyss. But with each sunrise, Perry chose strength, his spirit bolstered by a newfound resilience and a desire to write a different ending.

He emerged from the darkness not just as a survivor but as a beacon of hope. His 2022 memoir, "Friends, Lovers, and the Big Terrible Thing," became a raw and powerful testament to his struggle. He laid bare the depths of his addiction, the despair, the physical toll, and the unwavering will to overcome.

It wasn't a celebration, but a reckoning, a sharing of his vulnerabilities to help others find their own light. He wrote not with shame but with a raw honesty that resonated with millions. He wasn't Chandler Bing, the witty charmer, but Matthew Perry, a man who had walked through hell and emerged with scars and stories.

His struggle with addiction may have overshadowed his "Friends" years, but in confronting it, Perry emerged stronger, more compassionate, and more human. He became a reminder that even amidst laughter and success, darkness can lurk and that even the most devastating battles can pave the way for the most profound victories.

This is just one chapter in Perry's ongoing story, a tale of struggle and triumph that continues to unfold.

Chapter 8

Girlfriends and the Game of Hearts

Matthew Perry, the king of witty comebacks on "Friends," wasn't always all sarcasm and dry humor. Before he made millions laugh as Chandler Bing, his heart danced to a different rhythm—the rhythm of love, of stolen glances and late-night whispers, of relationships that unfolded both on and off the screen.

His love life, like his career, was a roller coaster of laughter and tears, brief flings, and enduring connections. So, let's take a peek behind the curtain, past the punchlines, and into the man behind the microphone as we explore the women who held a place in Matthew Perry's heart.

It all started with a secret—a whisper shared in a dimly lit corner while cameras rolled. There she was, Valerie Bertinelli, his co-star in the TV movie "Sydney," and sparks flew. Under the watchful eyes of her husband, the iconic Eddie Van Halen, Matthew and Valerie found themselves locked in a passionate make-out session. Was it just a moment of shared chemistry, a forbidden thrill? Or something more? In his memoir, Matthew confessed to harboring deep feelings for her, though their paths never officially intertwined as lovers.

Then there was Tricia Fisher, Carrie Fisher's half-sister, who swept him off his feet during the filming of "A Night in the Life of Jimmy Reardon." This was no on-screen romance; it was real, intense, and raw. They started young, both barely eighteen, and the physical desire whispered like the summer sun. Matthew, still the boy with a tennis racket in his dreams, tried to resist, to wait, but in Tricia's arms, logic lost its grip. Two months of yearning simmered over, and it was Tricia who took the lead, guiding their love into a physical realm. Their story, though passionate, had an expiration date, a bittersweet melody echoing through their later reunion years after "Friends" had taken over the airwaves.

Some stories are short, fleeting moments under the summer sun, like the "make-out session in a closet" Matthew shared with Gwyneth Paltrow, a whisper before the "Friends" storm hit. Others bloom like fireworks, bright and explosive, then fade into the night. Such was his relationship with Julia Roberts, a high-profile romance born on the set of a "Friends" episode. Laughter resonated between them, a shared love for comedy and good times. Love was in the air, and, for a few thrilling months, they were Hollywood's golden couple. But insecurities danced in Matthew's heart, whispering doubts, and eventually, with a heavy heart, he called it quits.

In the shadows of those public romances, quieter stories unfolded. Gabrielle Allan, a future writer of "Veep," became a witness to his early struggles with alcohol. She was there when the obsession first reared its head, a gnawing craving after a magic show, a feeling that would color his journey for years to come. But she was also a friend, a hand to hold, a reminder of life beyond the bottle.

Then there was Jamie Tarses, a woman described as "magical, beautiful, and smart," who stood by him through the depths of his addiction. She was a beacon of support, a shoulder to cry on, and a reason to fight. But when the battle grew too fierce, the battle he needed to fight alone, he knew he had to let her go. The path to recovery, he realized, was paved with solitude.

Some loves leave echoes, not just in memories but in unfulfilled dreams. Rachel Dunn, his "ex-girlfriend of his dreams," someone he dated during the tail end of "Friends," remained a bittersweet melody in his heart. Their breakup wasn't dramatic, just a quiet understanding that his focus, then, needed to be on sobriety. Yet, somewhere, a voice whispered "what if," a yearning for the path untaken.

The list goes on, each name a brushstroke on the canvas of his life: Natasha Wagner, stunning and perfect, a love briefly glimpsed; Cameron Diaz, a playful accident at a late-night dinner; and Lizzy Caplan, the six-year melody that almost became a symphony, a friends-with-benefits that blossomed into something deeper, only to leave him with a heart full of "what ifs" after their 2012 separation.

Finally, there was Molly Hurwitz, the literary manager, who stole his heart and held his hand in his darkest hour. A proposal in a Swiss rehab center whispers of forever under the European sky; their love story was a quiet haven away from the spotlight. Together for three years, but in 2021, their music faded, leaving behind a legacy of love and loss.

This was just one chapter in Matthew's life, a glimpse into the man behind the laugh track and the heart behind the sarcastic wit. And as the curtain closes on his story, we're left with a reminder that even the king of comedy has a heart that beats with the same messy, beautiful rhythm as the rest of us.

Matthew Perry remained unmarried throughout his life, up until his passing.

Chapter 9

The Ron Clark Story

In 2006, beloved actor Matthew Perry brought his talents to an unexpected role in the TV movie The Ron Clark Story. Though fans knew Perry best as the quick-witted Chandler Bing on Friends, this film offered a departure by showcasing Perry's dramatic skills as passionate educator Ron Clark. And much like Clark impacted countless students' lives, Perry's compelling performance left an indelible mark on viewers.

The movie depicts Clark's real-life journey from his small-town North Carolina roots to an underserved New York City public elementary school desperate for change. Rather than accepting an easier third-grade class, Clark insists on teaching the forgotten sixth-graders – rambunctious students already abandoned by another teacher.

What emerges is a poignant battle of wills between Clark and his class of misfits, outsiders, and troublemakers. The real test isn't boring standardized curriculum; it's about rediscovering the joy of learning by understanding students' individual stories first. Only then can real change take root.

At the movie's heart lies Matthew Perry, who brings Clark's relentless pursuit of connection to vivid life. Where a less capable actor may have rendered Clark as a caricature – either sanctimonious or hopelessly naive – Perry adds nuanced layers of humor, frustration, and lived-in resilience. It's a performance highlighted by quiet moments of revelation rather than big, dramatic speeches.

We see it in Perry's eyes when Clark finally earns a distrustful student's respect. Or his barely-concealed anguish when it seems his methods have failed, only to try again with renewed spirit. Perry makes it clear that this isn't about one man; it's about lifting up a community.

True to form, Perry generously provides room for his young co-stars to shine too. His interactions evoke a masterclass in listening, reacting, and elevating everyone fortunate enough to share his stage. In doing so, Perry creates something more profound than a one-man show – he helps construct a world where even the most underestimated young souls may discover their voice. By the film's end, just like Ron Clark rediscovers his higher purpose, Matthew Perry likewise reveals an untapped power within through this performance. No longer relegated to comic relief, Perry proves his worth as a leading man who uses charm to reveal greater truths.

Sixteen years later, The Ron Clark Story remains a testament to perseverance and believing in human potential – themes Matthew Perry clearly took to heart. Just as the real Ron Clark impacted an entire school, Perry leaves a legacy that has expanded far beyond a single role.

Chapter 10

Finding New Voices in Studio 60

As "Friends" faded to black, Matthew Perry wasn't ready to bid farewell to the magic of television. He craved a new stage, a platform to explore voices beyond Central Perk's familiar orange couch. This time, he stepped onto the vibrant, frenetic canvas of "Studio 60 on the Sunset Strip," a show that mirrored the real-life chaos and comedy of producing a weekly late-night sketch series.

Trading Chandler's sarcastic wit for the furrowed brow of Matt Albie, Perry took on the mantle of a beleaguered head writer and executive producer. Matt, haunted by past demons and burdened by the weight of responsibility, found himself thrust into the whirlwind of a network reboot. His partner in crime, Danny Tripp, a recovering addict played with raspy charm by Bradley Whitford, navigates the backstage drama with a mixture of cynicism and surprising vulnerability.

"Studio 60" wasn't just a backstage comedy; it was a pulsating commentary on the state of television, a world grappling with political correctness, celebrity meltdowns, and the ever-shifting tides of public opinion. Perry, under the masterful guidance of Aaron Sorkin, delivered a nuanced performance that transcended sitcom clichés. He captured Matt's anxieties, his flashes of humor, and the underlying vulnerability of a man trying to reclaim his creative spark.

The casting choices were a delightful cocktail of seasoned veterans and fresh faces. Amanda Peet brought sharp intelligence and steely resolve to Jordan McDeere, the network president, as he navigated the treacherous waters of corporate politics. Donal Faison, fresh off his "Scrubs" success, provided comic relief as a self-absorbed actor desperate to stay relevant. Kristen Johnston, armed with razor-sharp wit, injected the writers' room with biting humor and cynicism.

Each episode unfolded like a live wire, crackling with the energy of a ticking clock and the pressure of delivering laughs under the gun. Through sketch parodies and biting satire, "Studio 60" tackled real-world issues, from political turmoil to media bias, all while juggling the personal dramas of its colorful cast. Perry, at the helm of this creative maelstrom, delivered a performance that resonated with anyone who has ever faced self-doubt and fought for their artistic vision.

Despite its critical acclaim and passionate fanbase, "Studio 60" struggled to attract a sizable audience. Its nuanced humor and complex characters, while appreciated by critics, seemed lost on viewers accustomed to broader sitcom fare. After a single season, the curtain fell on the show, leaving a bittersweet legacy of unfulfilled potential and Perry with a new perspective on the fickle nature of television success.

"Studio 60" may have had a short-lived run, but its impact on Perry's career was undeniable. It proved his willingness to shed the skin of the sitcom king and embrace the complexities of dramatic storytelling.

Chapter 11

The Odd Couple

Matthew Perry had faced down sarcasm slinging friends, romanced neurotic lawyers, and even become a dog-hurling charmer for British audiences. But in 2015, he stepped into a familiar living room, albeit with a fresh coat of paint: the iconic apartment setting of Neil Simon's "The Odd Couple." This wasn't a rerun, though. This was Perry's own take, a modern reboot titled simply "The Odd Couple."

He slipped into the shoes of Oscar Madison, the rumpled, slovenly half of the duo. Felix Unger, the ever-meticulous Thomas Lennon, a comedic foil who could dust a sneeze mid-air. It was a reunion of sorts for Perry, returning to the sitcom landscape that had launched him to stratospheric fame with "Friends." This time, however, he wasn't just cracking jokes. He was the captain of the ship, co-writing and executive producing the show.

Walking the tightrope between honoring the beloved original and adding his own spin, Perry infused the series with contemporary wit. Oscar might still have a wardrobe best described as "a lost and found for bad sweaters," but now he sported a smartphone glued to his hand, a constant portal to online poker games and questionable late-night infomercials. Felix, ever the neat freak, was now a germaphobe with a Fitbit fetish, his organizational skills bordering on obsessive.

Their clashes were legendary. Oscar's messy cooking met Felix's sanitized utensils with the force of a culinary cold war. Felix's color-coded pantry battled Oscar's overflowing fridge in a symphony of mismatched Tupperware. Yet, beneath the bickering and pratfalls, there was a deep, if reluctant, affection. These were two men who, despite their differences, found solace in each other's chaos.

The show resonated. Audiences, both old and new, found themselves chuckling at the familiar yet updated humor. Critics, while acknowledging the shadow of the original, praised the duo's chemistry and the sharp comedic writing. For Perry, it was a return to his roots, a chance to revisit the sitcom format that had made him a household name, but on his own terms. He was no longer just Chandler Bing, the quip-slinging jokester. He was a creator, a collaborator, and an actor pushing his boundaries.

But this newfound stability was merely a blip in Perry's ever-dynamic journey. While "The Odd Couple" ran for three seasons, another creative outlet beckoned. Perry dusted off his own play, "The End of Longing," a deeply personal reflection on addiction and recovery. He took it across the pond, premiering it in London before bringing it back to New York. Once again, he bared his soul, proving that his talent wasn't limited to sitcom laughs. He could command both stage and screen with vulnerability and depth.

As the curtain closed on "The Odd Couple," Matthew Perry stood at a crossroads. He had conquered television, explored the theater, and proven his comedic and dramatic chops. But the ever-restless artist wasn't one to rest on his laurels.

Chapter 12

Cause of Death

On October 28th, 2023, the world awoke to distressing news. Matthew Perry, the much-loved actor behind the iconic sitcom character Chandler Bing, had passed away unexpectedly in Los Angeles.

As word spread, it was met with widespread grief and disbelief. How could someone so talented, who brought such joy and laughter into our lives, be gone so soon? Fans everywhere mourned the loss of a man who felt like a dear friend. Perry's former castmates also expressed their sorrow, speaking fondly of his warmth and humor.

In early November, several of his closest co-stars gathered somberly to say goodbye, highlighting the immense impact Perry had through his acting and his openness about confronting addiction. Shortly after, the Matthew Perry Foundation was started to support others struggling with similar issues, continuing his legacy.

However, one question persisted in the aftermath: what was the cause of Perry's untimely death? The answer came on December 15th and sent shockwaves across the entertainment world: a lethal ketamine overdose. Ketamine, an anesthetic medication sometimes misused recreationally, had reportedly been part of Perry's therapy for anxiety. Tragically, it seems his use of the drug led to his accidental overdose.

Overdosing on ketamine is extremely hazardous, often causing breathing suppression or heart strain. The coroner's report showed Perry experienced complications from multiple factors, including drowning, heart disease, and other addiction medications. But the primary trigger appeared to be a ketamine overdose.

This case underscores concerns around the growing practice of using ketamine therapeutically, which can help certain patients but has risks. Perry was unfortunately very vulnerable to these dangers, leading to irreparable loss. His passing stands as a vital reminder to carefully weigh the benefits and potential downsides of such unorthodox treatments.

Ultimately, Perry will be most remembered not for how he died but for the talent and spirit he brought to the screen. Despite grappling with addiction, he inspired many with his perseverance and maintained a reputation for professionalism and humility. His story was one of incredible highs and lows, reflecting the human experience.

While incredibly disheartening, perhaps some solace can be found knowing Perry's death heightened awareness around addiction and mental health struggles. If nothing else, more open dialogue around these issues may aid others facing similar battles. The best way to honor his memory is with more compassion and support for those still fighting.

Though gone too early, Matthew Perry leaves an enduring mark through both his acting and advocacy. May we celebrate the laughter and enlightenment he brought to the world while using this loss as motivation to carry on his efforts to help those in need. With more understanding and care, even more lives can potentially be saved, giving everyone the chance Perry deserved.

Chapter 13

Net Worth

From Humble Beginnings to Real Estate Mogul: Tracking a Sitcom Star's Climb to Riches

When Matthew Perry tragically passed away in October 2023, he left behind far more than just his legendary sitcom role. Equally important was the financial empire he had steadily built over decades in the spotlight – an empire reflected in his impressive real estate portfolio spanning glitzy mansions to sleek penthouses.

Like many Hollywood success stories, Perry's started small. Early on, as "Friends" rapidly rose to prominence, so did the cast's paychecks. By the last season, Perry and his co-stars were banking a staggering $1 million per episode, raking in around $90 million total for Perry. And thanks to backend syndication deals, the residuals kept flowing for years to come.

Joking after the first season that his initial L.A. home was a "shack with a leaky roof," Perry soon traded up for a luxurious $3.2 million Beverly Hills mansion in 1999. Showing his real estate savvy, he sold that property just six years later for nearly double the price of $6.9 million.

Over the next decade, Perry bounced between lavish homes, ditching Hollywood Hills for a $12 million Malibu beach retreat in 2011. Though he tried selling it for $15 million in 2020, it ultimately fetched $13.1 million – still a tidy profit. His largest splurge was a $20 million Century City penthouse purchased in 2017 and flipped to music icon Rihanna in 2021 for $21.6 million.

In many ways, Perry's real estate trajectory mirrored his eclectic personality – sometimes preferring the tranquility of oceanfront living, other times the electric energy of L.A. high-rises. And while numbers defined much of his empire, what truly mattered were the life experiences those homes hosted.

Perry leveraged his sitcom windfall to build an impressive portfolio, yes. But even more enduring were his willingness to take risks, his business savvy, and his penchant for bouncing back after life's downs. Combined with memorable performances still adored by millions, Matthew Perry's legacy extends far beyond dollar signs to something priceless.

Rather than focusing solely on his wealth, fans worldwide remember Perry for the laughter he brought into their homes. For shining light on addiction battles many endure privately. For rising time and again, no matter the struggles life presents. And for leaving an imprint on pop culture, few achieve that.

Matthew Perry's extraordinary life could hardly be captured by mansions or penthouse views alone. More importantly, he built connection, community, and comfort through his gift for comedy—riches that will outlast any property portfolio.

Chapter 14

Charity Work

While many fans will forever connect Matthew Perry with his beloved "Friends" character Chandler Bing, the actor cultivated an equally profound legacy outside the sitcom spotlight. Through tireless charity endeavors, he emerged as a champion for recovery and second chances—a role exemplifying Perry's depths beyond the screen.

Among Perry's most remarkable contributions was repurposing his own Malibu residence into the Perry House, a supportive facility for men overcoming addiction. By sharing this safe space of understanding, Perry provided sanctity and strength to individuals charting new paths forward. His dedication ultimately earned prestigious White House recognition, underscoring the facility's profound influence.

But Perry yearned to do more, laying plans for an eponymous foundation and broadening recovery resources nationwide. Much like a seed blossoming into a mighty oak, the compassion that defined

Perry House was poised to stretch far beyond Malibu, delivering hope to countless others in need of support.

Simultaneously, Perry has over 25 years of involvement with the Lili Claire Foundation, which aids children with neurological conditions. Through this longstanding bond, Perry spotlighted his drive to harness fame for selfless means, prioritizing humanitarianism over headlines.

Perry also joined forces with "Friends" casting director Leslie Litt on other noble ventures, their collaborative benevolence transcending professional ties. Though the cameras eventually stopped rolling, Perry's devotion never wavered, spotlighting nobility as the man behind Chandler Bing.

Additionally, Perry is credited with helping actor Hank Azaria achieve sobriety, demonstrating how small gestures rippled into redemption for peers. Through leading by example, Perry created a wave of influence that he may never fully recognize.

Perry even once lobbied Capitol Hill so drug courts could favor rehabilitation over punishment, underscoring his preference for guidance over condemnation. By voicing support for progressive change, Perry again acted as counsel for the struggling, not a judge.

Upon Perry's untimely passing, his "Friends" co-stars spotlighted not only his comedic brilliance but his immense heart – a dichotomy defining his essence. While the sitcom made him a star, benevolence marked his true legacy. The laughs he incited were matched only by the lives he touched.

While the Chandler Bing character will eternally elicit smiles in syndication, Perry's real-world acts of compassion form an even more profound legacy. Where Chandler was fiction, the Perry House stands as fact. Where Bing delivered punchlines, Perry provided patient ears and opened doors for recovery.

With selfless grace, Matthew Perry transformed entertainment fame into an amplifier for change. His home sheltered, his voice empowered, and his presence inspired fellow sojourners towards redemption. Long after the final bows fade, Perry's quiet crusade for human triumph persists – the greatest sitcom of a life well lived.

Conclusion

Matthew Perry was far more than his fan-favorite sitcom alter ego. Though indelible as the sly, sharp-tongued Chandler Bing on Friends, Perry's own story formed a rich tapestry, interweaving comedic brilliance with vulnerability and resilience. This dichotomy, evoking laughter and tears in equal measure, defined the essence of a man who transcended easy categorization.

Propelled by a childhood nourished on humor, Perry cultivated an early passion for performance. Though the path to stardom met roadblocks, Perry persisted through each setback and rejection. Every failed audition only sharpened his talents further, sculpting trademark comedic timing and a gaze perfectly attuned to satire. Until, at long last, fortune found him on Friends as Chandler Bing.

Yet great fame also casts inescapable shadows. As Perry's star rose to astronomical heights throughout the 1990s, he waged a private battle against darker impulses threatening to eclipse his vibrant spirit. The non-stop demands of celebrity placed overwhelming strains on Perry's mental health and sobriety. Still, even in such anguish, Perry's will remained unbroken. Time and again, he emerged from the ashes with courage and humor intact.

And while nothing could surpass Perry's small-screen dominance, he found creative outlets beyond Bing in other media. Reveling in dramatic work, theatrical pursuits, and writing, Perry proved himself a consummate and curious artist—one unwilling to be defined by a single role. Wherever he went, his signature earnestness and wit shone through.

In reflection, Perry's life echoed less some fictionalized script than it did a stirring Shakespearean journey: soaring high upon the wings of fame yet cut down by human frailties. But rather than tragedy, ultimate hope and enlightenment emerge. Because despite mighty personal demons, Perry leveraged humor as a shield against darkness, while exemplifying how vulnerability cultivates connection.

Though the curtain has fallen, the Matthew Perry legacy persists as a masterclass in courageous, authentic living. Not merely as Chandler's smirking ghost, but instead as someone who embraced the messy and wondrous spectrum encapsulating what it means to be human. Yes, Perry could elicit laughter from the depths of pain, but more critically, he reminded us that even imperfect lives can achieve perfect artistry.

The full accounting of Perry's rich experiences far exceeds any single chapter or book. But by exploring the extraordinary stories of others who similarly overcame adversity to leave indelible marks, perhaps their collective journeys can illuminate pathways through life's labyrinth for us all. Within each story lies emerging wisdom, elucidating the remarkable resilience of human spirits when faced with seemingly insurmountable odds.

Let Perry's courage stand not in isolation but joined by the chorus of so many voices once silent, now brought to song. And may the poetry found in those harmonies empower others still struggling to find their key. For in the end, it is the sharing of stories filled with both laughter and tears that makes our short walks here as wondrous as they are fleeting.

The stories don't end here! *Timely Press* has much more in store for captivated readers like you. Our expanding collection of fascinating biographies and motivating tales awaits on Amazon.

We welcome you to follow <u>Timely Press on Amazon Author Central by clicking "+Follow" on our author page.</u> This ensures you never miss a new release - whether it's a profile of courage, an inspiring saga, or revealing life story. There will always be another groundbreaking book to enjoy.

Thank you for joining Timely Press on this journey so far. With your continued readership, our chronicles will carry on.

- **Timely Press**

Made in United States
Troutdale, OR
03/01/2024

18108986R00038